JUDEAN DREAMS

Brandon Marlon

BAYEUX

Judean Dreams
Copyright © 2009 Bayeux Arts

Book design: Chris Shaddock
Cover design: Chris Shaddock

Published by: Bayeux Arts, Inc., 119 Stratton Crescent SW,
Calgary, Canada T3H 1T7, www.bayeux.com

Library and Archives Canada Cataloguing in Publication

Brandon, Marlon, 1979-
    Judean dreams / Marlon Brandon.

Dreams.
ISBN 978-1-897411-07-0

    I. Title.

PS8626.A756J84 2009   C811'.6   C2009-900746-0

First Printing: September 2009
Printed in Canada

Books published by Bayeux Arts/Gondolier are available at special quantity discounts to
use as premiums and sales promotions, or for use in corporate training programs. For
more information, please write to Special Sales, Bayeux Arts, Inc., 119 Stratton Crescent
SW, Calgary, Canada T3H 1T7.

The publishing activities of Bayeux/Gondolier are supported by the Canada Council
for the Arts, the Alberta Foundation for the Arts, and by the Government of Canada
through its Book Publishing Industry Development Program.

For all my forebears

Arise, walk through the land in the length of it and in the breadth of it; for unto thee will I give it.

Genesis XIII:17

TABLE OF CONTENTS

8 ROMANCE

9 REVERIE

10 PRAYER

ACKNOWLEDGEMENTS

The Canadian Jewish News, Poetica,
Yalla Journal, The Bulletin, Voices Israel,
Emunah.

MEMORY

Memories of the Modern Jew, I

Ship of the Desert

A wandering Aramean was my father
Who put foot to sand and stretched his legs pace by pace
Through the steam and earth

He crossed the Jordan and locals knew him as the River Man – Ha Ivri
His kin for a time could be found wearily toiling under Egypt's black sun
Habiru men and women bound in their hearts for Ashmem
After the gagging drought improved

Salem would have to wait for slavery generations and the mass Return
Of sandals and warm toes turning golden then rich pink

On sand dune ships of donkey and camel the tired souls
And burnt feet
Journeyed back to what by then was widely called Jeru-Salem
To rectify unfinished destinies and an ancient claim

A wandering Aramean from Ur was my progenitor
And I his wandering Jewish son am sorry my toes are so cold

Memories of the Modern Jew, II

Stranger's Torch at Jericho's Gates

A mob of slaves camped at Sinai's heel
To receive the world's gift and strengthen their backs
From the overseer's lashes

Tired eyes looked to the vast beyond from the nipple of Nebo
The transfer of leadership moving from prophet to general

High walls and massive towers confronted the nomadic rush
Canaan's siege a gradual affliction
Crippling the gates of fortified cities
While cousin cultures jostled for supremacy
And territory
And water rights

From all sides the devastating blows arrived –
Ammon and Moab raided swiftly from the West
And out of sweltering desert
Tribes of Midian and Amalek thrust with spirit and spears
To impale Hebrew faith

But for judicial strategists and the glow of Shiloh
The flame and legacy would have reached thick ash
Smoked into infinite invisibility

And I would not remember the texture of Samson's hair
And my ancestors would never have been pregnant with monarchy
Nor moistened by longevity's full-mouth kiss

Memories of the Modern Jew, III

Dynasty of Sin and Compromise

The reverberation can still be felt
Waves crashing into the coast of Canaan
Light tides ferrying heavy crews of Aegean skins

Preceded by a raging flame
Scorching the Fertile Crescent
Iron warriors and copper conquerors
Jeopardizing the boy nation of my grandfathers

Between Jaffa and Gaza
The search for allies and alloys was sparked a smoldering red

At the ensuing moment of immediate necessity
After beggary and protests: "A king! A king!"
The quest for solidarity in organization spawned a worldly throne
Pouring forth psalms for comfort
Proverbs for wit and wisdom
A dynastic line of Davidic ruler-saviors

Before long the tongue of Via Maris
Extended in branches throughout tribal villages
For traders in times of peace
For troops in times of caustic challenge

All for naught these assimilationist reforms
As ten pieces of Jacob's garment were torn
And centuries of subjugation and threat descend

Though the will will remain and the courage persist
Not the rising of any hammer clan
Nor any glow from sons of stars
Will lift up beaten root shards for good

▶

Two temples ploughed to dust
Zion City razed down to pebbles and embers
Baptism by inferno, drowned in sorrows
With but one memento wall
A die hard clinging to time and Moriah
For future fingerprints to be impressed
For buried ways to be unearthed
For all eyes to rise and look upon the faces of my ancient tribe
Still breathing and suffering
Outlasting Darwinian logic with inexplicable and undeniable exception

Come Closer *(Joseph)*

And he gave his voice over to weeping
Falling on their necks, tears streaming
All of Egypt heard, the entire domain of Pharaoh
He could no longer refrain, breaking down repeatedly
Until wagon met chariot in the land of Goshen
Till father and son were resurrected and reunited
Before death parted them once again and forever

Nicanor's Gate

An invisible crown anointed his head
This man of means with a Greek name
Whose heart belonged to the Hebrew god
Whose worldly riches followed his spiritual lead

Greater than a king, he kept a good name
That ferried his reputation from isle to shore
As his vessels plied seas for mercantile matters
But this man never forgot Jerusalem and Temple

The call came to him in Alexandria at last
Herod was restoring the Sanctuary itself!
Pledging his fortune to the Holy of Holies
He ordered doors of gold, silver and copper

With cargo holds and warehouses emptied
The purest elements refined to perfection
Seafaring merchant traded in commerce
Turning into pious pilgrim for the journey

Of all his vast fortune nothing remained
This master of fleets paid for his passage
And for his masterpiece doors to reach Akko
Eating only a bundle of dates for his meal

When sky darkened and sea grew rough
A howling wind tore through the sails
Frantic sailors heaved cargo overboard
Hurling treasures into water's angry mouth

Lashed to the deck and all that remained
The harried captain feared the doors' weight
With a mighty sailors' heave one door was away
Before its patron arrived in time to save its twin

▶

A special gilded cart decked with flowers
Awaited at port for the storm-surviving ship
The fame of the fine doors preceding them
Officers of Herod's court halved their hope

Suddenly a great billowing surfaced at sea
And spat out the door left for watery grave
Floating upon waves, brought gently to shore
It rejoined its companion en route to hilly Zion

There set in hinges before the innermost court
Stood the Temple gate leading to divine dwelling
When Nicanor saw his doors miraculously restored
His soul rose within whilst his heart burst with joy

Kannaim✡

Fundamentalist fighters with fanatical fervor
Vaulting with defiance at every enemy approach
Seventy years of resistance to Roman legionaries
Brought infamy and extinction to your fourth philosophy

Unlike the Law-lingering Pharisees, Sadducees and Essenes genera
Your turbid brand of politics was limited to sword and bowmanship
To the heuristic glories of besieged fortress and mountaintop suicide
Every Eleazar, Shimon and Johanan were felled by Italian sandals

Not even your Sicarii✡ could hold out forever under the impartial sun
That Silva and friends bent to will along with bursts of willy-nilly wind
Senseless hatred had long ago doomed your revolt to its predictable fate
You were as unfamiliar to unity as alien pagans to invisible monotheism

And in the end when circumcised bodies were set aside and counted
When choked cities with leveled walls again possessed food rations
Temple and capital were unalterably quenched by cold-blooded fire and
gladius✡
Only the Law poured forth bursting from the fount of Yavneh into survivor
hearts

✡ Hebrew: Zealots
✡ Hebrew from Latin: Dagger-wielding assassins
✡ Latin: The short, double-edged sword of a legionary

Sink for Dregs *(The First Revolt: I)*

The Temple became a sink for the nation's dregs
Every sin committed within its precincts
So that blood spilled from court to court
So that shame painted the pillars of every chamber
This was the work of the Zealot insane with grudge
Unqualified hatred and civil war acknowledging no immunity

And with no wheat for the rich
And with no corn for the middle class
And with no barley for the poor

Everyone felt the sword of starvation
As the savage rampage continued unabated
Madness and malady intertwined so that citizens succumbed

For when hunger reigns restraint is abandoned

The unthinkable becomes necessary, even routine
A holy city became a den of vice, a stronghold of sorrow
They drank each other's health in the blood of their countrymen
Unity squandered so that sanctity departed

Till there was no more room for all the crosses
No more crosses for all the bodies
No more bodies to relinquish life

Internecine strife destroyed country, city and Temple
Leaving only one lonely wall for the centuries to revere
For the collection of tears from two thousand years

Seven Species (*The First Revolt: II*)

Raging Zealots rejected foreign domination with fierce force
Sicarii sectaries went even further with swift assassinations
Sadducees were aghast fearing the forfeit of position
Pharisees quietly went along with more radical elements
Christians fled to Pella in the Transjordan
Essenes withdrew to the desert shunning perversion
Idumaeans in ignominy were tricked into Judaean participation

Seven species of partisan segregation dividing a nation
Each denomination narrowly sought self-preservation
Jostling for supremacy with little or no concern for one another
Turning a blind eye toward their own fellow brother
So that doom and gloom scenarios necessarily played out
Treachery and atrocity on display every day
A salacious spectacle of unbridled madness and wrath
A fallacious fantasy of conspiracy and unqualified mistrust
Red, red rivers overflowed street and alley alike
Power-hungry vulgarians locked in the vise of vice
Gripped by circumstance and hot-headed militancy

But now fate had decreed that one prison
Should confine the whole community
That a single city solid with men, brimful of corruption
Be held fast in bleak war's bitter embrace
The wholesale carnage of this destruction
The bottomless depths of these terrible misfortunes
Said to be deserved on account of the production
Of a generation so vile as to bring about its own ruin

Not one spot in the whole city was empty
Every single one had its corpse
Victim of hunger or faction
So foul a stench of human flesh greeted Roman conquerors
Though all scruples were silenced by the prospect of gain
While appeals for mercy spewed forth from the sewers in vain
For the window of armistice gave way to the closed door of parsimony
So fell Jerusalem on the 8th of Gorpiaios in the second year of Vespasian's reign

In Those Moments They Kneeled *(The First Revolt: III)*

The silver melted and ran, exposing woodwork to flames
Colonnades carried the fire forth
Porticoes caved in, toppling in turn
When the Jews saw the ring of fire
They lost all power of body and mind
They stood looking on in utter helplessness...

A work of art sanctuary condemned to conflagration
By the turning of time's wheel the fated day had now come
A soldier without orders urged on by some unseen force
Snatched up a blazing piece of wood
And climbed another soldier's back
Hurling the firebrand through a golden aperture...

As the flames shot into the air
The Jews sent up a calamitous cry
Ears were deafened by a great din
Amid the distractions of battle and bloodshed
Among smoking ruins and slaughter and flight
Round the altar the heap of corpses grew higher and higher...

Down the Sanctuary steps poured a river of blood
Bodies killed at the top slithered to the bottom
There was no restraining soldiers, no arguing with fire
In the iron embrace of battle the flames roared past persuasion
Many who were wasted with hunger and weak beyond speech
Now found sudden strength to moan and wail at the top of their lungs...

The cries from the hill were answered from crowded streets
Back from the mountains round about came the echo in thundering bass
The Temple Mount boiling up from its very roots
A sea of flame meeting an ocean of blood
Panicking priests threw themselves into the fire
Dutifully perishing amid the relentless blaze...

▶

And as the limestone exploded from overheating
As the Temple crumbled gate by gate by gate
In those moments the Jews kneeled where they stood
On surrounding hill and in narrow valley they fell to the ground as one
Tearing their garments, dousing ash upon their heads
Screaming and weeping, groaning and begging for the face of redemption...

The Road to Masada

Brown, brown road with trail blazed by ancient sandals
Sacred stronghold in sight within the night
Boulders line the roadside for late traffic
But we are daylight trekkers in need of a different help
We seek out ancestors and ghosts of battles past
With every step I hear Josephus whispering
And I whisper back: "Was it exactly as you say?"
There the conversation ends as the distance nears
And the citadel's presence takes over completely
Desperation and doom, a mystery immortalized desert-style
Nothing is written in stone despite its omnipresence
What I know for certain is that atop a certain mountain fortress
Remains the remains of a synagogue sanctuary
And by sunrise next I'll have its walls against my hands
With a passionate Kadish✿ between my lips

✿ Hebrew: Memorial prayer for the dead

Mar Zutra✿

Persian oppression forcing his unripe hand
An Exilarch of exception arrogated autonomy
Carving a kingdom for his kinsmen
As a deposed autocrat bewailed incarceration

With four hundred fighters the task was tenured
Seven years of Semitic sovereignty ensued
In the throbbing epicenter of an empire
Under the auspices of the scion of the House of David

Yet diasporic dominions were unsanctioned
Immorality corrupted freedom-rich followers
Beheaded hung the bodies of the renegade and relatives
Suspended from crosses on the bridge at Mahoza

✿ Leader of Persian Jewry, circa 496-520 C.E.

Courageous Qurayza✿

Woe and alas to the Israelite Alamo!
O, you martyred males of Medina
Priestly tribesmen loyal to ancestral leanings
Yathrib farmers of fidelity and independence
Quraysh and Ghatafan✿ pagans could not uplift you
From the clutches of the new conquering creed

Surrounded and betrayed in the overheated Hejaz
Heroic resisters massacred by the hundreds
Rather than accepting the yoke of Arabian epiphany
Widowed women and urchin children sold into slavery
Radiant Rayhana alone found favor in warrior-prophet pupils
Which more than once acquiesced to youthful Jewess bounties

✿ One of three Jewish tribes in Medina in the era of Mohammed
✿ Arab tribes opposed to nascent Islam which unsuccessfully attacked
  Medina in 627 C.E.

Judaism Means Rebellion

Some sacrificed their children to Moloch
While others prostrated themselves before wooden Baals
Yet he refused abomination in favor of the Most High

Some built cities as dens of corruption and vice
While others burnt villages to punish the weak
Yet he erected walls to shelter sanctity

Some grew vast empires by conquering their neighbors
While others capitulated to oppressive occupiers
Yet he neither conquered nor kept quiet under foreign yoke

Some lived by artificial regulations suiting oneself
While others waxed philosophic by the wisdom of each new theory
Yet he governed himself by the morals and ethics of the Almighty

Some speak without filter shaming tongue and lips alike
While others behave cruelly, outdoing each other's insensitivities
Yet he watches his tongue lest he shame his Creator

Some demonstrate profound contempt for piety
While others taunt and mock the righteous few
Yet he cultivates a refined demeanor worthy of his ancestors

Because Judaism means rebellion as all can plainly see
Because Judaism means rebellion (or at least it does to me)

In the Tent of Nomads

Great decisions are taken amid humble surroundings
Immense undertakings initiated by willful soloists
Like Lawrence and Aaronson entwined in turmoil
One never possesses ultimate awareness of the moment
Until deeds and doings are long preserved in posterity

Oh, how much Fate is in so little!

A meeting of minds or crossing of thresholds
Only reveals its significance or irrelevance
At the harbor of hindsight's lighthouse tower
In the crystal clarity of retrospection's late hour
When the dust has settled, caked and cracked
And none but deceased participants own the details

TRADITION

Ketubah✿

My red brother in blood
My coated cousin of many colors
My kindred mate in modern-day fate
Is there a ketubah in your future?

Parchment, ink, gouache, tempera and gold powder
Ancient words in portal motif
Iconologia and family crests crowded by floral patterns and watercolor
Metallic paint greasing your name
Along with that of your bride
Your new lasting pride
In ceremonial attire of a Yemenite:
Dress, headdress, robe and leggings
Pearls, coral, and silver,
Ten necklaces/Ten bracelets/Ten rings
One large smile and infinite glimmer in the fountains of her eyes

If perhaps, if so,
Let it come that day
And let me stand first in line
To dine on kosher wine
And drown my jealousy away

✿ Hebrew: Jewish marriage contract

The Mantle of a King

With beaker and goblet I toast a modern David
That you remember and cherish the deeds of your namesake
His haggadah✿ of works and sins
And be blessed with a maiden in Miriam's form
Featured with a seder✿ plate of varying virtues
Whose hands are always full of challah✿ loaves
Whose lips are dessert wine of cherries
Whose neshama✿ spouts forth soft words to comfort you
Whose breath is a spice box as if for havdalah✿ time
Whose fingers are exquisite like bronze menorah branches
Her candlestick arms and whose eyes will be a Sabbath lamp
For weary days and shadowed nights
Whose life reads as the Scroll of Esther
Be aware of the old stones of your ancestors' ruins in faraway Jerusalem
For there lies earthed a crumbling clay jug of wine
With your royal Hebrew name scratched in its skin;
Do not leave it buried for it waits in secret still for your mouth alone

✿ Hebrew: Tale—the Passover storybook
✿ Hebrew: Order—the Passover ceremony
✿ Hebrew: Braided loaf of bread eaten on the Sabbath
✿ Hebrew: Soul (feminine form)
✿ Hebrew: Distinction—prayer ceremony with which the Sabbath ends

Oil Lamp for Yom Kippur

I found an oil lamp in Parur, India
Bronze, eighteen inches, circa 1670
Originating in the Cochin Jewish community
Whose custom was to keep it lit all day
On Yom Kippur

Though the lamp looked Indian
The letters were those of Jeremiah
And Ezekiel
No djinn✿ in this gizmo
No matter how hard I rubbed

Amen, let us be judged in the light
Let the Lord decide our case
Searching a clear face
Let us be judged in the light

✿ Arabic: Genie—traditional spirit of Arabian lore

Between

Dreaded weekday interlopers
Interfering with sacred Sabbaths
I loathe your secular style
Offending the holy haven of the seventh day
Weekdays are my useless lovers
Keeping me from my Sabbath bride
Blessed be our Lord who differentiates
Between holy and mundane
Between the sacred and the profane

Shabbat✡

You promised to come
Though I knew you would leave
You left me alone and I could not help grieve
I knew you'd return – I knew in my heart
Full faith in your virtues I kept from the start
Your visits were brief
It could only be so
I long for your presence wherever I go
I anxiously await your sunset arrival
I need what you give for my spirit's survival
And when again you depart
And make way for a while
I'll think of you quietly, and often, and smile

✡ Hebrew: Saturday, the Jewish Sabbath

Fire & Wine

Two candles on fire
One design-carved cup overflowing wine
Swaying witnesses to kiddush✿ in tune with its tune
Plucked from the antique Ashkenazic✿
And seraphic Sephardic✿ repertoire
As braided challah loaves tangle together under cloth
Like conspicuous lovers under their wedding canopy

However strong it comes on
Havdalah always has the last say
A stretching braided candle whose twist is flamed
Its light reflecting in nail mirrors on fingertips
While its loyal red libation accomplice
drips from the same silver cup
kissed by kiddush hours earlier

This is marriage in the time-honored fashion

✿ Hebrew: Sanctification—the prayer over wine recited on the Sabbath
✿ Hebrew: Judeo-Germanic
✿ Hebrew: Judeo-Hispanic

Menorah Men

Eight places to be filled by great flames of guidance:

Abraham/1
The first of us to surrender heavenly bodies for the Almighty's supremacy

Moses/2
For leaving the royal house and leading impoverished mud slaves

Isaiah/3
For railing and ranting like a madman at the wind to serve his impenitent people

Judah the Maccabee/4
For fighting back against the Hellas stranger's Hellish hand

Hillel the Elder/5
For his uncommon sense of compassion and moderate mentality

Bar Kokhba/6
For lifting his nation from their knees and a world empire from its shoulders

Maimonides/7
For his mind's complexity and his heart's sentimental suffrage

Theodor Herzl/8
For willing an exile's buried dream onto the map and lost tribesmen back to their homeland

And in the 9th place, the caretaking Shamash✿ who introduces and ignites all others
I place universal justice
Without whom the heroes are not heroes
And the memories unworthy of remembrance

✿ Hebrew: A synagogue's beadle, and the middle candlestick on a menorah from which others are lit

Man of Midrash✡

In the shadow of the masterpiece tome
Under the influence of its mace-like clout
A modern scribe toils in tales of old
Layering legends upon venerated precedents
Advancing the story a few paces into contemporaneity
Revitalizing and rejuvenating fable afresh
Bridging lacunae history left open in silence
These are the territorial waters wherein possible and plausible joust
The land of maybes and what ifs come alive
Fact and fantasy thrive in matrimonial bliss
And myths procreate from kernel seeds of veracity
Blossoming and blooming, branching out toward infinity

✡ Hebrew: Traditional legend

Mine Are Counsel & Wisdom

As Avram and Sarai, proselytes of old
You too may have a ה✡ added to your name
If you move away from sin and draw near to merit
Moral power exercises control over speech and behavior
The Law can be your savior
A healing to your body
Marrow to your bones
A graceful garland for your head
A noble lace for your neck
When you walk it shall guide you
When you lie down it shall guard you
And when you awake it shall speak on your behalf
Its adornments protect, its attributes instruct
The way has been shown us
Wisdom and will must be supplied
For our life and joy to be multiplied
Its path must be tread free of coercion
The reward is in direct proportion to exertion

✡ "Hay"—the fifth letter of the Hebrew alphabet, equivalent in sound to an H

Crown of a Good Name

Neither may we explain the tranquility of the wicked
Nor the suffering of the righteous innocent
But is it not better to tail the lion than head the fox?

With reputation bound at the stake before all
We prepare in the lobby to enter the banquet hall

With modesty, humility and tact in abundance
A loyal gentle wind will follow our footsteps
Our presence will be a pleasant fragrance
Our aromatic aura will be met with affectionate warmth

For against our will were we born and will we die
For we are the branch of His planting, His handiwork
In our deeds and doings will He take pride

We must retain dignity and maintain integrity
If esteem is to be sustained in the eyes of our fellows
If regard and repute are to enable and endear

The three crowns of Torah, priesthood and kingship are tall
But the crown of a good name surpasses them all

A Song to the Ascents

I raise my eyes to the desert mountains
From where will my help arrive?
To the Rock of Jacob, the Shield of Abraham
Will I look for deliverance, goodness, grace, compassion
Lauded, upraised, mighty, extolled, exalted, glorified, praised and blessed
Be the name of the Holy One
Not in any man do I put trust nor on any angel do I rely
But to his glorious and holy name do I declare praises
To his greatness and strength, splendor and triumph
Rock of the Eternities, Shield of David
May He remember the covenant of the spiritually mighty
May He help, shield and save all those who take refuge in Him
You who cling to the Almighty are all alive today

Aish Tamid✡

Eternal fire ever glows
Reaching higher the flame grows
Up to Heaven its heat ascends
As a nation makes amends

✡ Hebrew: Eternal fire

Torah

It is a tree of life for those who grasp it
It is a fertile field for those who sow it
Its ways are of pleasantness and its paths of peace
Its supporters are praiseworthy for their pious strivings
It is a crown of salvation for those who wear it
Its righteousness is like the mighty mountains
Its gifts are endurance, serenity and contentment
It fills your stomach and swells the mind
It provides spiritual strength to prevail over adversity
Sponge, funnel and strainer will each fail
But you can be its sieve if you truly believe

Division's ✡ Tradition

Every enlightened generation of Jews
Has its Mattityahu and Menelaus
Its Judah Maccabee and High Priest Jason
To contend for the national will
With right hand cunning and oratory skill
When the majority must choose
Between Hellenist and Hasmonean
Israeli and Israelite

The Sons of Jacob are like the Western Wall
Small stones of secular modernism creeping up
Layered on thick slabs of religious boulders
Each column and row in need of the other
To ascend skyward and keep out the profane
While stifling the invasive mundane
That would infiltrate the crevices of faith
Like a wiry weed permeating moisture-concealing cracks

The long Hebrew hour ticks into eternity
In spite of seductive millennial trends
Coursing through the stringent body of tradition
As if a mutating antigen fleeing a pursuing antibody
That flaunts immunity against the ages

Shikkuż Shomen✿

Don't look now, Daniel!
Handovers
Pullouts
Security transfers
It's enough to excuse
Our hiding out
in the Diaspora
When, I wonder...

Turn away, Hasmonean!
World opinion
International pressure
Un resolutions
When, I challenge...

Adjust your view, Zealot!
Even Human rights
Even Peace
Can be made into idols
To be worshipped blindly
No matter the crooked cost
When, I question...

Close your eyes, Bar Kokhba!
Giving, giving, giving up
what is rightfully one's own
A modern abomination of desolation
When, I demand...

▶

will Maccabi✡
mean more
than a beer
a soccer team
a sporting competition?

For who needs an Antiochus Epiphanes
an Hadrianus Augustus
with fashionable liberal cowardice
and guilt-laced self-hatred
doing their work instead?

✡ Hebrew/Aramaic: Abomination of desolation
✡ Hebrew: Strike—moniker of the Hasmonean hero Judah ben Mattathias
and his followers

Jewish Quarter

Square stones brightly bleached by the sunlight of three thousand years
Glossed with the moisture of lips and tears salting away the oversized rock surface
The optimum kingdom has itself eroded much over time
Wrinkled like a dry raisin through the ages from its original grape cluster
Cane-dependant inhabitants hobbling along cobbled meandering alleyways

The harp replaced by the haunting wail of sorrows tallied in collective sufferance
The walls of the calcified capital rose and fell like a seesaw abused by hyper children
Things have not gone as planned for the People of the Book
If you take a good look
As if Heaven disengaged from the Chosen unilaterally long ago

So it rests with the competent curious to excavate dirt and rubble
Praying in ancient languages to discern the way back to a time of favor
When towering Temples stood seemingly forever
And the greatest enemies of Israel were not established innately within
Tanned Hebraic skin
The Sabra✿ has again and lately lost its prickly exterior for all but its own
As the arch nemeses stitch rival flags and rally victory's chants
Readying the conclusive strike against a hopelessly divided tribe
Lost to its initial savior shepherd

In the faded jaded Jewish Quarter
The slumbering number of an ancient age
Ratifies itself another day by virtue of its ongoing degeneration
While its prospects dissipate like a city gate before Roman siege machinery

It seems more and more that not for long
Will Zion's song have a throat to horn it proudly
Only sad violins will contemplate the painful dirges of what might have been
Had kin stuck by kin

▶

Planting modern shoes in dusty sandal prints of impassioned ancestors
Instead of surrendering to imperial pressures in contemporary guise

Here stand Jacob's progeny at truth's moment with eager foreign eyes aglow
Straining across continents for a better view of self-immolation on Jehovah's
cracking altar
A taunting refrain looping in resenting minds
Mellah, mellah✿, mud-brick and wall
Who's the eldest of them all – but soon historic relic!
An ironic revenge enacted before their seedy sight
The Israelite people on its sacrificial deathbed carefully laid out
Finally headed the natural way of the fossilized Philistine
The pounds of patrimony too burdensome for shekel✿-seeking slacking
shoulders
Collapsing at the first capricious waft of world opinion's irresistible breeze

---

✿ Hebrew: Cactus—slang for native Israeli
✿ Arabic: Jewish quarter
✿ Hebrew: Currency of the State of Israel

In Israel

They asked my purpose of travel
I spoke to them of my ancestors

They inquired where I was planning to stay
I related to them scriptural passages in detail

They queried me as to the duration of my trip
I admitted to them many lifetimes

They thought I was in Israel
I told them Israel was in me

MYSTICISM

Ancient Aims

As the Ark among the Philistines
I am uncomfortable in my surroundings
I have no sefira✿ to make manifest divine dexterities
And I don't believe in God small 'g'
But I trust soft words over a platinum amulet of Yahweh/Adonai
Elohim/El Shaddai
Though I love the sun nuzzling my face
More than exegetical and homiletic materials
I will glance at the statuette of a bearded man from Uruk
To seek Sumerian insights in case
I am the primitive one
After all, it is Khufu, Khafre and Menkaure
Who have pyramids in death while in life I have yet to possess a modest town-
house;
A sphinx guards their domain and I lack even a goldfish
If your throat is dry perhaps the ancient world has arisen in your mouth
And you will need the Nile to slake your Tigris-like thirst

✿ Hebrew: Sphere—kabbalistic term denoting a number in the chain of
the realm of God's manifestation

The Spirit of the Five Voices

From the cup of blessing shall we sip
A joyful taste of the wine of mirth
The birth of happiness continually celebrated
Gladness and glee will coat our hearts
Breath from elated lungs will inhale contentment

As the groom from his room peers out to the sun
While the bride exudes pride as final touches are applied
With congregants gathered from all walks of life
Forgetting their strife and defeats and frets
All eyes ascend from lonely individual affairs
Combining as one they merge sans seam

Alert and attentive to the voices all about
A spiritual clamor transcending all spheres
Illuminating dark years of long ago and just lately
Sects are sequestered and factions are felled
Dissipated into nothingness as unity prevails
Barriers torn asunder even as walls are rebuilt
A people submerged resurrects hand in hand
In solid matrimony with the master maker
With vim and resolve unseen for ceaseless centuries
Unheard of since soft whispers from the central shrine abated

Then will grace and gratitude overflow
Seeping through cracks in calcified hearts
Ruins and remnants will heave desperate sighs
And the vibrant vow of ages will find resolution
For when again the Temple altar sings its scented smoke to the sun
Hear, O Lord, Your people of Israel is one!

Pulsa Denura✿

With these carefully archaic Aramaic utterances
Pronounced in the hazy heat of righteous rage
I call down Biblical wraths with a whip of fire
Eradicating irascible infidels vexing tradition
Cause for suspicion and counter-positions

I tongue out this curse to cut down and reverse
The infuriating maze of manic treachery
At a moment of lashing lechery
Disloyalty to the founding fathers of faith
Repaid with persuasive prayers venom-cloaked

Divide my house and I must kabbalistically cast you out
Excommunicated to the realm of next-life clarity
Before pillars of cloud and pillars of fire will we testify
For you have given the lie to our holy heritage
Sacrilegious acts staining your brittle bones

How shall you withstand the blast of my vitriolic vow
Slashing away your see-through imprecations
A thunderous oath undermining criminal blasphemers
Honorably attesting against illicit travesties
Mocking perversions of our esteemed patrimony

So that your concession is not my sacrifice
Your appeasement not my children's burden
Your turnabout not my brethren's bane
Nor my descendants' debt in harsh perpetuity
One malicious hymn taking us back to dark desert days

And like armored Crusader knights in chivalric duel
We shall nobly allow the Almighty to judge
In the crimson clear terms of imminent blood
Whose favor He now graciously attends
From whom He expects eternal amends

✿ Aramaic: Lash of fire—a mystical curse

Sambatyon✿

Dust and sand and waves of fire
Spewing rock of boulder and pebble
Passionate currents prohibiting trespass
To exiled northerners subjected to Assyria

Waters of obeisance inclined to the divine
Raging and resting according to schedule
Nature synchronized to scriptural injunction
Cloud and clamor ceasing only on Sabbath

✿ Legendary river in the Near East crossed by the lost tribes of Israel, which
ceased flowing on the Sabbath

ADMONITION

Lone Immigrant

Absorbed into difficult surroundings
Friendly face nowhere in sight
He walks the days and reflects the nights

Cats and garbage pollute sacred streets
Moving to the blaring beat of honking horns
Unknown universes die quietly as others are loudly born

The help that he hopes for falls perfectly flat
Prompting the search for fresh angels tonight
Loneliness seeks consolation in clouded starlight

Shy Guy in the Land of Chutzpah

Reticence does not reign
Hesitation proffers pain
Here in the land
Where chutzpah was born

Passive, civil and polite
Gets you nowhere in a flash
Among high-volume car horns
Among vibrating hand gestures

Only audacity writ large
Conveys messages plainly
Here in the land of nerve
Where abnormal is de rigueur

With the gorgeous at the hilltop
With those grubby at the base
Here in the land of garish gall
Where burekas✿ and rugelach✿ rule

✿ Hebrew: Stuffed dough pastries, otherwise known as knishes
✿ Hebrew: Miniature chocolate croissants

After Hours in the Holy City

They belong to the night
Denizens of dark encounters
Citizens of once upon a time sin
Liberated by shadow and starlight

Cenobites absent amid the youthful throng
Which bears no semblance to sanctity
Which seeks no halo of holiness
Nighttime everywhere classifies morality as an expenditure

Israeli Politicians

Sergeants of surrender
Captains of capitulation
Admirals of appeasement
Lead a split nitwit populace to doom
One bomb and rocket at a time
On Heaven's chosen dime

Lefty antics of self-destructive smut
Collapse dreams of other brothers
More in tune with self-love than self-hate
Enough to make an Israel-lover irate
At the grossly ignoble state of the State
That nowadays looks to be a finite experiment

Jews need a righteous Judge or pious King
A poetic Prophet and humble High Priest
Leaders who are clear, bold and decisive
Un-plagued by modern moral ambiguity
Unencumbered by self-defeatism and stupidity
Willing to stand their ground *on their ground*

I hope I live to see that very day
I wish for it privately as others pray
But no breath will be held for such drastic change
For such a radical fantasy far out of range
Elected Israelis are but fools of the hour
Lacking the longevity of a higher power

World Opinion

Condemnations from left and right
An international community aghast
Excoriations with no end in sight
A tiny Nation deprived its great past

The whole world cannot be wrong
Goes the latest greatest UN refrain
Corruption's chorus stoked in song
Sad gathering of the institutionally insane

One State surrounded, kicked to the floor
Resolutions drafted to make us all safer
Democracy perverted, abused to its core
One-sided vitriol not worth the paper

Never Again! is hummed the world over
But the entire world is yet again blind
Inertia and apathy a noxious power
Resulting in atrocity when combined

Around the corner, could you believe?
Haman's newest despicable incarnation
Another six million for whom to grieve
If conscience fails swift resuscitation

With the power to act fingers fell numb
Limb went limp when it counted most
For Rwanda and Darfur senses kept dumb
The whole world fast asleep at its post

▶

A complacent world wallows in ambivalence
Partisan and self-serving, lazy and cold
Illegitimate by virtue of moral equivalence
Far from a welcoming place to grow old

Attacked all around with weapon and lie
Prospects increasingly appearing grim
A lowly Nation voices Heaven-high
Avinu, Avinu, shehba shamayim...✿

Whatever will be in the end to come?
Weeping mankind never in the know
The One and Only possesses the sum
...Tzur Yisrael v'Goaloh!✿

✿ Hebrew: Our Father, Our Father, who art in Heaven...
✿ Hebrew: ...Rock and Redeemer of Israel

Modern Eyes in Zion

They will roam Ben Hinnom's Vale, but will they gaze upon Moloch's dead
babes?
They will hike the curving Kidron, but will they recall Jehoshaphat's desperate
angst?
They will excavate the City of David, but will they swoon to the strumming of
his harp?
They will peer into dark cave depths, but will they behold doomed Zedekiah's
dire peril?
They will follow lengthy timelines, but will they appreciate Jeremiah's time-
lessness?
They will recreate golden Temple vessels, but will they recognize Maccabean
heroism?
They will climb the Tower of David, but will they sense lonely Herod in Pha-
sael's ruins?
They will stroll the Way of Sorrows, but will they feel the prick of the crown of
thorns?
They will look up at lofty Scopus, but will they see cohorts of grumbling
legionaries?
They will caress ashlar stones longingly, but will they smell the roasted burnt
offering?
They will unearth ancient coinage, but will they appreciate Bar Kokhba's
weighty sword?

Once Upon a Time in Jerusalem

Once upon a land there was rolling greenery till the horizon
Trails that propped up pilgrims' feet as they ascended
Presently there are broken roads strewn with rubbish
Only identical black pellets of camel dung recall yesteryear

Once upon a people there was inner faith and outer mirth
Contented souls appreciative of familiar comforts
Today there be mass disillusionment and property angst
Only shadows of holiness slink through Old City alleyways

Once upon a time Jerusalem was a city worth fighting for
Defending and dying for if necessity irrevocably ordained
Nowadays precious little remains of contested remnants
Only scraps of history gawking at chaos from stone graves

Olive Drabs

Their jacket darker than their pants
Shades of olive all the same
Coursing the country in pell-mell helter-skelter fashion
In jeeps and on buses, through field and desert
Battalions maneuvering in mock battles
Between genuine repeat engagements
A nation defended by green youth in verdant vestments
Plucked from their branches some seasons before ripening

Gates Decayed

Grungy and grimy
Are the gates of Zion
In an age beyond their namesake

And I sense increasingly
That my century has been missed
By but a mere millennium or two

Rock and rubble
Clutter the Holy City's face
Like centuries-old stubble
Grass creeps out of rich soil
Masking mounds of yesteryear

Crows fill the skies
While fat felines prowl the streets
Whimpering for more strictly kosher leftovers
Swirling and sniffing at saccharine garbage
Smells emanating from open dumpster heaven

Ashen caves pock the valleys
With untold histories
Hills hide their Semitic secrets
From disruptive roadways
Carrying by oblivious denizens
Brimful of ignorant contentment

Sirens in the Streets

Wailing three at a time
Red motion in rhyme
A sign of stillborn discourse
No international intercourse

Death by the dozens
Dispensed among cousins
Blood by the puddle
First responders huddle

Terror ever timeless
Bottling human kindness
Tragedy as the headline
By daylight or moonshine

Chant Down Jerusalem

Retailing ancient notions from this merciless jungle
Quaint concepts fall short of lasting impact
Fissures in the deception are rife and unmistakable
Presumptuous polis of cement-hearted citizens
Thick with kings of aggression and queens of insensitivity
Prophets of corruption and status quo standard bearers
Bureaucrats empty of all efficiency stifle necessities
Religion chokes sanity in institutional fashion
Secular residents gag for oxygen in secluded spaces
Blaring car horns readily scream human insolence
A capital bankrupt of kindness and contemptuous of civility
Renders archaic Babylon aloft in comparison
From out of Zion the message still goes forth
Though lacking sincerity's stamp it is returned to sender

Lonely Man of Faithlessness

They abnegate and abjure with finality
Renouncing reason in favor of communal tradition
Absolutists of doctrine, dogs of dogma
Having no truck with the sin of uncertainty
Nor countenance for the heresy of scruples

With nary a wind to scatter his doubt
Alone is he among the guarantors of destiny
Never having known the serenity of surety
Forced to chose between blind reliance or else defiance
To distinguish between conscience and convenience

He is no god's patient witness for he believes what he sees
Some fall in love with phantoms; others with wraiths
Bleeding and broiling in honor of ancient idols
Common sense conclusions direct him to one derivation:
God is the lullaby orphan children sing themselves

Yet how can belief be sheer sustenance to some
While simultaneously seeming as utter denial to others?
Philosophical fractures inevitably segregate searching souls
Leaving but two types to thrive in the Holy City's midst:
Those blissfully delusional or bitterly disillusioned

Makeshift Society

Careening city buses imperiling unsteady elders
Speeding cars taking unnecessary chances
Armed forces with Samson-like hands tied behind back
Party-ocratic political coalition system with advanced multiple sclerosis
Sleepy storefront security guards bored into early graves
Rudeness as a revered value permeating society
Concessions to sworn enemies from a position of no identity
Sub-basement standards in urban execution
Caustic ingredients forming a recipe for extinction
Nothing fails like failure nor disables like disability
With anything goes as the order of the day
'It'll be all right' (or at least so they say)

REDEMPTION

Paideia✡ Judaea

Epode and eclogue
Proclaim in its name
Whether attributing the source
To human reason
Or divine will
Moral action is memorialized
Accent on the ethical imperative
On the ethos of brotherhood
And the commonwealth of mankind
An expression of humaneness
Will not suffice to describe
What is in fact
Imitatio dei

✡ Greek: Perfection through kindness

Kadosh✡

Tikkun Olam✡ is not enough if you only look elsewhere
Avoiding with concentrated care those bitter wars within

Beneath the spin-making skin of the matter lies the battle at hand
That repeatedly begs and demands urgent priority resolution

Will we not atone and repent to Man and Heaven both
For the broken oaths and forsaken vows of moments ago

Holding the mirror to oneself so that flaws lose their stealth
Is incumbent upon the sincere seeker of pure redemption

So when casting the net throw it straight up over your own head
In order to confront the unkind impulses that provoke wrong

What living being will never succumb in moments of weakness
Who would deny that the fruits of reflection require earnest addressing

Beware the ignoramus who excludes contrition from his list of core needs
The Master needs no Yom Kippur to know the true nature of one's deeds

---

✡ Hebrew: Holy
✡ Hebrew: Emending the world (i.e. social reform)

Raya Mehemna✡

Feed the right grass
To each type of us sheep
So collectively we render
The wide-worshiping world
A devout dwelling place
Where Heaven feels comfortable
Lesson and legislation
From the passing-through People
For whom even their Oral Law
Was carefully transcribed

When a birthright is one's background
Heritage one's honor
No task is too vast
No destination too distant
The call is for now
The call is for all

Faithful Shepherd
Take the high road
God-fearing person
Come after your wayward flock
Collect us tenderly
Return us in mercy to Jerusalem

An enormous task
In an orderly fashion
Redemption from erstwhile exile
To apprise the eyes

▶

Of mind-blind nomads
Appraising visceral visions
Freshly arisen
And like Joshua
Servant of Moses
Neither shall we budge
From our teacher's tent
Though dashing desert sandstorms
Whistle heavy-handed winds against us

✿ Aramaic: Faithful shepherd—Talmudic term applying to Moses

Disparity

Between Jew and Israeli lies a maturing machtesh✿
A canyon of unfamiliarity now well-confirmed
But I affirm this must end in our lifetimes, friend
Some are complacent in the face of this gap
Feeling helpless when tasked with bridging the gulf
Nevertheless a start is well worth making
With painstaking care for Hebrew souls everywhere
Come into my sukkah where fine wine awaits
Come under the chuppah where promises are made
Let's lift up a tallis✿ high above our kippot✿
Let's roam ancient ruins and ponder their stories
I'll gladly sing Hatikvah✿ while you smoke on nargileh✿
If you drink from my kiddush cup and hold the candle for havdalah
Land and Exile should be close enough to whisper
For it hurts me to raise my voice from my side of our divide

✿ Hebrew: Crater
✿ Hebrew: Jewish prayer shawl
✿ Hebrew: Skullcaps
✿ Hebrew: The Hope—the Israeli national anthem
✿ Arabic: Water-pipe device

Facing East

Imagination's muse lusts after a world heavy with destinations
Each more enchanting and historic than its predecessor's spectacular standard

When I look to faraway eastern shores sucking on Mediterranean seawater
I can see millennia of antiquity unfolding in fleshed characters and divine-
handed events

I ponder the role my fingerprints might play in this ongoing tale of wonder
and woe
The story of Jacob's progeny has many parchment scrolls yet to be pain-
stakingly inscribed

When I cast a glance Jerusalem's way I sense the toll of days
Piled on the city's plowed back slouching in staunch valleys and hilltops

We come from tanned eastern origins goes the rumor mill still
But by now I fear the Red Sea water has evaporated in my Westernized ears

When the biers of time carry off the weights of tragic yesteryears
The lessons and warning cling to three-dimensional relevance for literate
moderns

Halevi nearly made it, almost-almost as they now offhandedly say
His dream bequeathed to generations of exiles Diaspora-weary

When even today the devout in their synagogues pray
Eastern-bound hymns in honor of Zion's grace-kissed mounts

I look to my feet turned outward to Old World ways
And think of days distant when Bible plots were breaking news

Zion Be Born

Zion is not a place, so fold up your map
Look not with the eyes but rather the heart
Picture a community where love is binding law
Imagine a society careful with words, considerate with acts
Sensitive to all creatures and nature alike
Brotherhood and sisterhood rejoicing in equality
Where the only throne is occupied by the seat of unity

Zion is not an epoch, a golden age long ago
That passed us by without so much as a hello
It's not something to get back to post-haste
Rather to implement anew for everyone's sake
Thought, word and deed have lasting effects
Respect must not be rationed as if a scarce resource
But spread far and wide with sincerity and pleasure

Zion is no slave, neither to time nor to space
The limits of human mercy are its only chains
So let thoughtfulness reign as mankind's refrain
Neighbor to neighbor with comfort for the stranger
That orphan and widow find solace from sorrow
That the poor are sustained and the oppressed witness justice
Zion is surely a destination, whose only road is loving-kindness

I Have a Dream

I have a Judaic dream
It takes place early on a warm Shabbat morning
In the Holy Land of Israel
Throughout the land the streets are empty
Every synagogue a packed house
Every mouth forming part of a collective voice

In Jerusalem above all the air is congested with prayer
Crowded Temple precincts are the order of the day
The Levitical choir chants in unison
Melody and harmony blend to praise God eternally
While tranquility reigns in the hills, valleys and fields

Serenity abounds wherever the brilliant sun shines
Minds are at peace
Hearts are overflowing
Spirits soar skyward
All because Man walks humbly with his Maker
As attending angels look on with envy

In the Eyes of an Exile

With a mystical reverence for the Land
Responding to primordial prayers and ancient aspirations
I went up to the heights of the elevated East
Faithfully expectant of a visitation of salvation

My turbulent heart endured steep highs and lows
Spiritually I flew and fell even within the same hour
Yet that could not sour my hopeful beliefs in a better day
In redemption or reconciliation or the powers that may

Still in all things I attempt to retain a smile
It may yet be a while, in the eyes of an exile...

Elegy for an Enemy

Down, down, down you go
To meet the hard pit of your affliction
Justice's extended arm now grips you
In a death lock beyond escape

I dare not gloat nor even smirk
For the fact you died my foe is our common woe
Mutual failure to overcome odds and differences
A joint social wrong never to be righted

And now, alas, our chances have passed
Our strife is ended and our enmity broken

Consider this, then, a token of regret
Mere modern musings to alleviate a parched grief
Yet I gladly recall wiser words of long, long ago:
Who is mighty, strong and brave in the end?
He who makes of an enemy a friend!

LANDSCAPE

Negev Nights

Instruct me on the stars
And strum the smooth guitar
This desert knows no pain for lack of rain

Bonfires and meditation games
Out in this faraway station
Rumors of scorpions circulate like cars in roundabouts

Tents haphazard — some more than others
Songs of the state and bluesy tunes
The broken silence under bright crescent moon

Night in the Negev is a Jewish howl session
So instruct me on the stars
As the smooth guitar strums anthems alive

Steel Birds

Two-by-two they pair across sky and cloud
You see them before you hear them
Steel birds in overhead flight
Crunching stones beneath your feet
Jagged cliffs scarred by water wounds
Negev days under noon's blistering sun
Chased by sound in silent soar

Steel birds know a different kind of hunger
They want for the freedom of swooping flesh
As the eagles glide in arching curves
As crows and vultures dive for their lizard lunch

Spreads of Seduction

Hummus, tachina and baba ganoush
Conspiring triumvirate of ubiquitous dips
Like childhood chums attached at the hip
Ready to be kissed by bread's soft flesh
All set to seduce tongue and cheek alike
I dream of a bonfire, whole wheat challah to spare
I dream of the night's fresh desert air
With hummus and friends, even a bowl of charif✿
With Ishmael and Mohammed and Omar Sharif

✿ Hebrew: Pungent—a spicy red pepper dip

Speak to Me Softly

Speak to me softly of the desert's raw flesh
Of its rise-and-fall skin of chalk and stone

Speak of the sun's merciless kiss
From cloudless blue-sky bliss at high noon

Speak in the mother tongue of external visions
Conjured on a sweltering trail with water running low

Speak of the bold breeze escaping across the landscape
Fleeing through a carpet of sand to heights unknown

Speak not of figurine idols whose clay cracks with time
But of eternity's vivid majesty reigning above and below

Speak with your eyes and bone and teeth
Let your words scratch and claw and bite their hearers

Speak for the eras and ages
Crack the quietude and set the silence on fire

Speak to me in the language of rock
That I may never forget your timeless words

Sons of the South

Ours is a beige solitude by day
A black isolation by night
Starlight sight sessions rewind
The myriad of morning events that impacted
That made a dent in the mind's paradise

The landscape's silence is a runway for reflection
The visual vista feeds cognitive hunger
Every new notion an oasis of imagination
Each sudden perception a mental meal revealed
Wasteland wilderness bears its share of creative genesis

The desert is a shelter for life-weary wanderers
Negev nights delight those daring or else lost
Its darkness is not frugal, its barrenness benevolent

The north has gone forth and has filled its mouth
While we still feel the famine as sons of the south

Salt Flats Syndrome

Salt flats syndrome in full effect
I stress the broiling pressure cooking my thoughts
And again I am at a loss before unfathomable beauty
Realized in real-time vision precision
I'm faced with the indecision of where to look
What path to follow or carve
My mind won't starve with the risen dream lingering all around me

Even though I blink it never goes away

It stays so long that I am woefully outlasted
If not for the water I would have fasted my body into submission
Surrender is no option in these saline valleys
The desert gives no quarter as a matter of order
It is happy to punish everyone equally in good measure
As a toll for experiencing its rarified treasures

Though it cannot be offended the desert is ever unforgiving

Tel Arad

Castle fortress on rocky hill
Temple terrace with view of the plain
Sacred rites in careful chambers
Canaanite and Israelite exhumed together

Stone and chalk climbing high
Ibex and lizard scurrying about
Pigeons in formation swoop down a well's depth
Caves and carcasses with tales untold

Bedouin gatekeepers hungry for shekels
Army base firing range makes itself known
A babbling brook slinking down slope
Tomato farmers tending multi-colored fields

The long arm of the law stops at the desert
Where the law of nature takes over
Night in the Negev belongs to the elusive scorpion
To the burgeoning moon glowing afar

Lookout

Five eagles circle overhead in freestyle formation
As the desert landscape reveals itself before me
I sit and scrawl where Judaea and Negev mesh their stone flesh
Where the sun heats the wind that blows by below and on high
Where mountains fold and stretch as they please
Chocolate-brown rocks terrace the beige hillsides
That rise with a crunch like biceps of Samson and Goliath
An occasional fly buzzes by just to remind me he's alive
The distant ranges and horizon make promises vague yet ambitious
But what if anything does the faraway mist conceal?
Is it illusion or might it actually be real?
Canyons and valleys with labyrinthine appeal
So surreal
Yet in fact I already know what secret the desert guards with its life
Like a jealous husband would a seductive wife
It is the answer to spiritual strife
A place so safe from all interruption
So remote its existence is mystical
Free from even ubiquitous fighter jet and tour group
From snake and scorpion interloper
From bird and beast, man and machine alike
It is silence alive
It is peace of mind
Where the only disturbance is the sound of your own heartbeat
And you have half a mind to snuff that out, too

Into the Desert

I go into the desert in a hurry
But I leave the desert very slowly
The desert is holy
For in it is found peace
In its pristine silence serenity blossoms
And for once I can hear the sound of a breeze
For once my soul rests with the quiet as a lover

Like a shot fired from the sky's own bow
A squadron of birds in arrow formation soars
With the unmistakable roar of unity
The wind is the desert's whisper
Humming in passing murmurs
A holy language all its own
Natural and magnificent and bewildering

Take me in, I beg of it
Surround me with your stony solitude
Envelop me in your earthy embrace
I am in your flesh yet I leave no trace
Though your influence on me no force could erase

The Desert Speaks

The desert speaks through its blustering breeze
The mountains speak from many cave mouths
The clouds speak through their shadowing shade
The sun speaks with its luminescent light
All of them say "Praise God with your spirit and soul"
Worship our Maker who breathes and shapes life
Who darkens and illumines our world

Green Carpet

She appeared overnight to decorate the desolate floor
Coloring the surrounding ground with verdant vibrancy
A lush coating of post-winter vividness unveiled
Layering the familiar beige and brown with springtime splendor
Hill, valley, plain and crater equal beneficiaries
Of the wilderness' seasonal benevolence
As if the desert were beautifying herself in preparation
With nervous perspiration
In anxious anticipation
For her lifelong lover the summer

Stones & Bones

The deserts of my ancestors are littered with remnants
Lingering proofs of their sojourns through limestone time
These rocks made of epic events and sagacious sagas
Speak in hushed tones of conclaves and battles
Of love affairs to resuscitate and resurrect the lovelorn
And of passionate concern for the welfare of the Land

It staggers the soul to conceive of the lucent role
Played out on history's stage by simple forebears of faith
Who in their eras walked about in cloaks and sandals
Muttering humble prayers and tenderly planting fields
The yield of my people exceeds their flesh and landscape
The stature of their sacred rapture surpasses the masses

Jaffanomenal

Once upon a time there was a beautiful beachfront city
A paradise in turmoil during the 1930s riots
Yet ever charming and picturesque
With a sense of subdued semi-seclusion
Her waters are striped and spotted in different hues of blue
A mist surrounds her as if she is mystical
Church, steeple, minaret and clock tower
Attest to her inclusive, elusive power
Her labyrinthine streets are an amazing maze
I am caught up in a mellow rapture daze
Port of ports, harbor of harbors
I could live within her as certainly
As she has always lived within me

Haifa, Amen

Layered city of angles and amity
Perspectives abound in this town of plenty
Terraced gardens on sloping steps
Beautify the land as it faces the bay
Naval city at the navel of northern splendor

Blessed with art and natural magnificence
My eyes could not get enough of you
I yearn to know your hills and alleyways
Your staircases and tales of bygone days
Accept my praise so sincerely proffered

Rushing on wet streets past your secrets
I know I must spend quiet moments lingering
Capturing your picturesque essence piecemeal
Or in a single, prolonged devouring
Though you have been bombarded your heart is tranquil

With communities engaged and mixing
Blending to better serve, sustain and preserve
The vibe is alive with hope and resilience
Haifa's brilliance is open coexistence
Society shared is society unimpaired

Beyond the Sea

Somewhere, beyond the sea
Tiberias waits there for me
She glows at night atop her hill
In rocky garden Galilee

Galil✡

For my turmoil and hard strife
Thou art sweeter than a wife
You help me wait and see
You red wine of Galilee

Through valley and through height
You provide me strength to fight
Never giving third degree
O rich wine of Galilee

How I sip your gentle kiss
All the others I dismiss
You know how to let me be
Dark red wine of Galilee

On your taste I do rely
For a calm and blissful sigh
To your prowess must I flee
Good red wine of Galilee

Against your spell who can resist
To all your virtues will I list
Your good name is safe with me
O pure wine of Galilee

When ancestors bid me forth
Senses quickly bring me north
Now go on and set me free
You red wine of Galilee

✡ Hebrew: Galilee

Galilean Greatness

Gilboa boasts in greens, browns and yellows
White cube villages nestling among rocky hills
Down below cars move along roads like ants in a line
Like red flowers sprouting from grassy mountains
Are moments of pure peace amid regal nature
Seldom spotted but of surpassing beauty
Random and rare like an ancestral ghost in broad daylight

JERUSALEM

The Approach to Jerusalem

Terraced hills left, right and center
Overwhelm senses despairing from such beauty
No wonder the world competed for this city
Nestled on sloping mountains as far as the eyes see
You can't believe this stratified town from a distance
Only in her belly can she be properly perceived
Hurt your feet exploring her numerous realms
Earn deep soreness discovering her domains
Drench yourself in fatigue patrolling her paternities
Your spirit will leap and bound even as your legs give out

City of Salvations

In the quarter of Justice law and order reign
Equality governs with systematic rule

In the quarter of Peace serenity blossoms
Tranquility blooms with placid tolerance

In the quarter of Fellowship fraternity flourishes
Support and encouragement build friendships that thrive

In the quarter of Love mercy dominates
Compassion patrols with forgiveness arresting wrath

Holy City Home

O Jerusalem, how unlike any other!
If I were you I would blush red
At all the words written about you
At all the lyrics singing your praises

Every sojourner entered your gates
And explored your ancient wonders
Every army has been your lover
Some more gentle than others

You are nothing if not resilient
In the face of epic epochs
Your hills are ever alive
With melodic sounds of sanctity

I extol you in the East
As I exalt you in the West
I lift my eyes to greet your face
I touch your walls with ten thousand thoughts

For this generation's Jew, wandering still
A few words offered in the spirit of goodwill:
Though I hope you will travel and faraway roam
I hope more that you'll call the Holy City home!

A House of Prayer for All Nations

Gathered under one canopy the assembly bustles
Briskly sidestepping passers-by from near and far
Distinctions fuse in fast-paced processions
Cobblestone streets teeming with intensity
Merchants and mystics, prophets and poets
Intermingling seamlessly with the pious and righteous

A wall, church and dome occupy mutual vicinity
Some days they share while others they compete
Four seasons of passion unravel the years
The burdens and tears born of happenstance and havoc
Concentrated chaos and exploding tensions
Periodically revived rivalries over time, space and legacy

But through it all psalms and hymns rise heavenward
Whispered in private or wailed in public
All proffered humbly in the spirit of hopeful goodwill
By weepers and seekers of a living god of love

For His house is a house of prayer for all peoples
And His mercy is most abundant and everlasting
Such that it is not even a question of us or them
Rather we must all pray for the peace of Jerusalem

Jerusalem of the Heart

A siren of a city, a nymph of a clime
Her beatitude resides in resilient ruins
With great charm in her crumbled loins
Masses congregate to imprint fingertips
To whisper and wail hoping to prevail
Still the times are not yet in favor
The hour remains far from ripe
Lonely towers and widowed walls attest
To history's duress and the scars that mar
But what aged queen could dare to compare
With a royal maiden in the prime of her reign?
Human fulfillment is Heaven's to sustain
To the Most High I pray time and again
Fill us with piety and wisdom and sense
Plant us on the straight path with a gentle push forward
That collectively we move toward redemption
Doing to our fellows as we'd have them do unto us
Loving our neighbors, making ploughshares from sabers
For it's high time to stand out, to make a fresh start
It's high time we built the Jerusalem of the heart

Romantic Love by the Western Wall

A pair of religious lovebirds alone late at night
Sweet couple sitting and speaking softly in the dark
Exchanging deep thoughts and stealing quick glances
Pouring out their bursting hearts and hopes for the future

Together yet separate they listen and learn modestly
Hours slip by as they smile, wink and sigh
'Could this be the one?' they wonder to themselves
'God, let this be my one and only, once and for all'

When their private encounter eventually concludes
They rise from their quiet corner and stroll home
Unbeknownst to them their rendezvous has been recorded
Witnessed and preserved by bright stars and heavy stones

In the Tomb of the Prophets *(Mount of Olives)*

Triple prophet crypt with Christian additions
Catacomb jungle complete with flashlight and rope
A French monk attends to assist and converse
His helpfulness is equaled by his talkativeness
In the Parisian tongue we discuss Christ and the Maccabees
In terms of modern, popular lore fed the masses
He regales me with the history of Celtic Saint Brendan
Bidding me adieu with parting words of luck
"Man of God" he calls me as I make my way out
Knowing Jew and Christian are close family even still
Seekers of truth hoping to illumine dark caverns
Yearning to reveal ancient secrets of stone and dust

Tombs of the Sanhedrin

I doubled-over to inhale a whiff of your chilled bones
Braving the petrifying potential of sudden snake attack
My feet disturbed the garbage collected amid your shaded dirt
As my eyes peeked into niches of your taciturn crypts

I came after your wraiths to absorb legislative legacies
To instill reverence for sagacious spirits and judges of the Law
You were not around and must have left your dusty gray graves
No longer at home in neglected tombs turned to wombs of rubbish

Starry Night in the Valley of Hell

How cool and harmonious is Hell tonight!
Quiet valley strip dipping low to meet Kidron✡
This much-maligned ditch of Gai Ben Hinnom✡ so lusciously rich
Caressing the western ridge of Old City splendor
The stars are out in full force this night
To my fortunate delight I am greeted and awed
By brigades of sparkling pockets of light dotting black sky
With youthful music wafting past to double serenity's magic
It's a whole new world of romance and exciting chance
Possibilities for the future dance around the hall of my mind
I want to rewind these moments of enchantment and replay them often
In love with the mysterious potentials I drift along disavowing Heaven

---

✡ A dry valley east of the Old City in Jerusalem
✡ A grassy valley west and south of the Old City in Jerusalem; its name
contracts to Gehenna, i.e. Hell

Stars Over Silwan

On the wrong side of the winding Kidron
Peering out toward the City of David
Residents of this hill warily weigh life chances
Carefully considering options and soberly seeking out opportunities

Up the steep slope anxious neighbors deliberate
Consulting one another about the latest prospects
Down below children shout in the streets in the midst of soccer
Unconcerned by the calamitous qualms plaguing their preoccupied parents

Another afternoon slips away from yet another dismal day
Dry like the valley are the inhabitants' dreams
Only the odd wayfarer interrupts the monotony
Until sun sets on their communal chorus whose helium hopes rise with the
stars

I Am Jerusalem!

I am the tireless subject
Fluttering ten thousand tongues
I am the picture painted
By master artists in each generation
I am the muscular mounts
The voluptuous valleys
The cobblestone remnants
Beneath pilgrims' precious feet
The underground tunnels
Propping up millennial layers
I am beloved by prophets
By high priests and saints
I am the markets and accents
Coloring public squares
I am the city of David
May his name ever reign
I am the cave and the crypt
The name inked in script
I am the blood spilt in crevices
The sweat on the brows of my defenders
I am the symbol and the thought
Not extinguished with the Temple's fire
I am the blaze in the hearts
Of my loyal rememberers
I am rolling hills and high walls
That so loftily arise
In the sparkling pupils of admiring eyes
I am the golden crown and its diamond gem
Eternally, I am Jerusalem!

ROMANCE

Blessed Pairing

Long, long ago
And far, far away
There came a time
Yes, there came a day

Man met his match
His one, one true love
He had some help
From high, high above

Soulmates in sight
Oh dear, dear good Lord
So deep, deep in love
Their spirits just soared

Then, then they joined
And went hand in hand
Now, now at last
United they stand

Oholibah✿

My tent is in her; and I will come home
Her arm bones and leg bones are its poles
Her sheltering almond skin its colored canvas
Her blood the warming fire to thaw bitter cold nights

My table is her flesh; and I will sit to feast
Her thighs are luscious cushions to dispel weariness
Her shoulders firm pillars of a fine banquet hall
Her teeth the shining candelabra lights to reflect in chandelier eyes

My chair is her embrace; and I will hold on tightly
Her knees are posted knights guarding my comfort
Her hands soft cantaloupes caressing my limbs
Her clasp the solid shell tenderly enveloping its coconut

My plate is her face; and I will eat fully
Her cheekbones are an altar to comely offerings
Her earlobes plump figs to swallow whole
Her hair the lengthy herbs of an aromatic spice garden

My meal is her soul; and I will consume spirit
Her words are honeyed cakes that melt within
Her joyous laughter refreshing oasis water
Her silence the serene desert wilderness I yearn to roam

My dessert she hides; and I will discover it
Her breasts are fresh honeydew of the field
Her toes batches of grapes for nibbling
Her tongue the soft mango slice whose juices slip fast and flow

My liqueur is her sweat; and I will inebriate myself
Her heartbeats are swellings of a ripe pomegranate
Her sweetened lips moist palm dates
Her breath the fertile earth inviting my warmth

My tent is in her; and I will come home!

✿ Hebrew: My tent is in her—a Biblical female name

Machanibah✿

My camp is in her, rock of refuge
Her borders offer safe haven
Her presence shelters the weary
Her stronghold secures the wounded

My will is her gift, shield of strength
Her smile its own reward
Her laughter a benevolent boon
Her soft nature a sweet dessert

She is the port in my storm
A hiding place from my pursuers
She is the lighthouse in my night
The ransom from my long captivity

My camp is in her, my seas she calms
With her my spirit rests well
Mah tovu ohalecha Yaakov!
Mishkenotecha Yisrael!✿

✿ Hebrew: My camp is in her
✿ Hebrew: How goodly are your tents, O Jacob! Your tabernacles, O Israel!

Eshet Chayil✿, S.O.S.!

As ordinary as a triple eclipse
As common as cold fire
She teases from uncertain fate

Encountering her is salvation
Clothed in the image of desire
Her breath inflates senses
Her touch incinerates innocence

Queen of your karma
She will defeat all doubt
Batter stout defenses
Lay siege to your soul
Take your skepticism prisoner
Enslave cynical misgivings

Her arsenal is loyal comfort
Her gift is righteous support
Best believe your city will fall
At the knowing blink of her eye

Giving in never felt so ordained
Surrender and seek terms
Throw open your gates
Like a peasant on his knees
Desperate for fate's fulfillment

✿ Hebrew: Woman of valor

Helpmeet

A dress of fire will clothe her
Burning you even from afar
Sun and moon are in her eyes
Effervescent like precious metals
Hers is a brilliant skin made of stars
Glowing with the aura of Providence
Luring you in with the magnetism of the inevitable

Though she speaks in subdued whispers
I hear her like thunder over the sea

Her kiss is the taste of lightning
Her absence deafens like winter rains
Her arrival impacts like a meteorite
Her breath alone will knock you to the ground
Sparkling flashes emanate from her fingertips
Her mysterious magic is fortune's supernatural zenith
Brace yourself for fate's energized embrace!

Jewish Attributes

I call out to you like a prolonged blast from the spiraling shofar✿
I reach up to you with outstretched arms like the branches of a menorah
Caressing your delicate skin like a yad✿ touches holy ink letters
Wrapping my fingers carefully around you like soft tefillin✿ straps
Blanketing you with warmth as a tallis from head to toe
I unravel your mysteries like a parchment scroll of Law
Devouring you voraciously like a braided loaf of challah
Imbibing you like an overflowing kiddush cup of wine
You are supported in my embrace like wax in a candlestick
For you I am ever sturdy and stalwart like a Western Wall
Bursting with hymns and prayers like a machzor✿ on high holidays
Since you are my Shabbat I will compose a siddur✿ of love songs in your honor

---

✿ Hebrew: Ram's horn
✿ Hebrew: Hand—the silver pointer for following while reading from the Torah scroll
✿ Hebrew: Phylacteries
✿ Hebrew: Special prayer book for the High Holidays
✿ Hebrew: Regular prayer book for the Sabbath

Married Flesh

I'll wash ashore along the littoral of her lips
Stumbling about the beach of her face
I'll chase her breathing with my eyes and ears
Honing in on her heartbeat to learn its rhythm
Loving her with tongue and eyelash and fingertip
Exploring every secret crevice for its hidden wonders

Her thighs will be fresh canvasses
On which I'll impress a masterpiece
Gently will I lay my head down
In the wadi between her breasts
Plotting strategy to conquer surrounding hilltops
Before dawn exposes the full scope of my siege

Beloved

Like white snails
On beige desert floor
You are everywhere
And forevermore

Like painted seashells
On cool Jaffa beach
I see you all over
And soon within reach

Embedded

I am in you like a crumpled note
Tucked into a Kotel✿ crevice
Like each folded piece of paper
I will only be extracted from you for burial

✿ Hebrew: The Western (Wailing) Wall

If Walls Were Made of Letters

If walls were made of letters
They would be interpreted not battered

If they were built out of hope
The world would display deeper sincerity

If they were constructed from kindness
Their ramparts would stand fast forever

If walls were erected out of love
They would melt to the pilgrim's touch

In Terms of Love

In terms of love, there's too much to say
And not enough words to say it with
In terms of the heart, nothing's for granted
It runs its own course, like it or not
In terms of affection, it needs a willing target
A clear direction to aim for and reach
In terms of faith, it rests well with love
Believe in the power that conquers the hour
In terms of hope, just keep looking forward
Straight ahead fate awaits your confidence
In terms of desire, forever remain its master
Passion overpowers and overwhelms the inexperienced
In terms of pain, which can't be escaped
Learn its lessons that polish the soul
In terms of spirit, always renew and refresh
Refine to revive then rejoice in its resilience
In terms of Heaven its one road is love
Nothing else nears us to the One above
For if God isn't love, and love's not His sign
Then He isn't really God, at least no god of mine

Of Almighty Love

If all the heavens were parchment
And all the reeds quills
And all the oceans ink
They would not suffice to record love's depths!

If all the earth was a canvas
And all the rivers flowing paint
And all the trees brushes
They could not suffice to portray love's splendor!

If all the wind was my breath
And all the sand my words
And all the stars my spectators
They should not suffice to proclaim love's eternal praises!

Please God

Please, my God, if it be Your will
Grant me some mercy, and more mercy still:

Let me find someone who loves me...
Like the sky loves its height
Like the mountain loves its rock
Like the earth loves its soil
Like the ocean loves its water
Like the desert loves its sand
Like the sun loves its light
Like the moon loves its glow
Like the stars love their sparkle
Like the river loves its current
Like the road loves its pavement
Like the rainbow loves its color
Like the bird loves its flight
Like the wind loves its air
Like breath loves its oxygen
Like touch loves its feeling
Like I will love her...

Touchstone

Like a golden inner altar of incense
She is an awakening and worthy of reliance
I see myself playing twenty-two strings of her harp
The seven strings of her lyre won't suffice or satisfy
I'll need all ten to memorize her rhythm inside and out
Knowing her nature is cause for merriment and mirth
On that day of resplendent revelation and joyful jubilation
I'll blow silver trumpets from the tower tops at dawn
Blasting joy to the four corners and four winds

Inner Altar

My love for her is like an Aish Tamid
Eternal heat of ever-elevating flames
Resistant to dousing by external means
Persistent and persevering despite difficulty

Burning with renewed daily dedication
Blazing with a hungry, heartfelt determination
Is my adoration for the object of my affection
Steadfast and stalwart as a wood stove in winter

Regular sacrifices take place within me
Atop my inner altar of dependable devotions
In internal courts of amorous emotions
Flooding with a most relentless conflagration

Hearts Aflame

Love is double-sided like an angel of fire
Disguising its edges as the prince of desire

Opening one's heart is like releasing a stream of fire
Flowing and flooding amid straits that are dire

The pain of yearning is like stones of fire
Building and climbing like flames on a pyre

Heaven's voice resounds with shafts of fire
Roaming and rising ever higher and higher

Temple Three

Ezekiel imagined architecture
But all walls fall in the end
Better to build the heart's sanctuary
Lover to lover, friend to friend

Woman of Valor

Come now to me, woman

That I may sit you down before me
And wash arched feet in rosewater

That I may pour perfumed oil
To anoint smooth-skinned shoulders

That I may caress soft-flesh neck
With loving, nimble fingers

That I may bury my face
In supple pillow breasts

That I may taste tender, honey-date lips
And measure soft thighs with cream kisses

Daughters of Jerusalem

Dressed in radiant raiment
Anonymously borrowed
You danced in vineyards
In shining fields of Shiloh

Fluttering from fresh breezes
Chanting songs honey-voiced
White gowns spun in the wind
Even as the sun swiftly plunged

Embraced now by cool night
Flirtatious festivities lingered
By torchlight and bonfire
Angelic figures swayed alive

Spectator bachelors eager and awed
Beckoned forth by your charms
With your wide, sparkling eyes
With your wide, blushing smiles

Landscape of Love

Your face glows like sunrise over the Golan
Your hair is rhythmic like waves of Galilee's sea
Your eyes are deep like craters of the Negev
Your lips are luscious like orange groves of Jaffa
Your breath is moist like winter rains in Judaea
Your breasts are perfect mounds like Herodium and Betar
Your arms are sturdy and durable like the walls round Akko
Your hands are soft like the soil of the Jezreel
Your thighs are curvaceous like the winding Salt Sea coast
Your legs are slender and elegant like cypresses of the Sharon
Your feet are arched like the gates of Temple Mount
Your skin is smooth like the banks of the Jordan
Your wit is razor sharp like the peak of Gamla
Your temper is tempestuous like wind over Masada
Your spirit is lofty like the heights of Haifa

And, like the Land of Israel, I will love every part of you

Sanctuary

With sparkling eyes like golden gates
With lofty cheekbones like upper balconies
With warm breath like billowing altar smoke
With sweet voice like harmonizing Levites
With soulful sighs like priestly benedictions
With moistened lips like pure oil in the lampstand
With arousing perfume like fragrant frankincense
With firm limbs like sturdy towers
With smooth thighs like polished white marble
With long slender legs like pillared colonnades
With fiery flesh like seared sacrificial offerings
Your blessed body is the sacred Temple
And your heaving heart its Holy of Holies

Love Is My Nationality

My nation is love
My statehood is mercy
Beyond borders and customs
My territory is goodwill
My people are citizens of forgiveness

In my heart of hearts
Hatred has no passport
Ill will faces an uphill battle
Wherefrom battalions of warmth
Breathe down fires of tenderness

We Shall Kiss

We shall kiss, you and I
Like Hinnom and Kidron
Winding our wadi tongues
Into seamless connection

Your lips press against me
As if I am your menorah
For night after night
They blaze me alight

Old City Swooners

Cisterns full of love
Kept shaded and cool – like ol' Bethesda Pool
As a general rule: Ecce Homo! – Behold the Man!
But I beheld your brown Judean tan
When you brought chaos to order
Down deep in the Jewish Quarter
Then we met once more through karmic fate
Right outside teeming Damascus gate
Destiny's date smiled upon us yet again
Warm moonlit nights on the Street of the Chain
Regards to St. James who witnessed love-struck power
When we touched at that very late hour
My loins pulsed higher than even David's Tower
We French-kissed in front of poor Sister Maria Sosa
Strolling along dark Via Dolorosa
And now when I whisper your precious name
Cathedral and hospice are put to shame
You will be my Terra Sancta
Walled in on all sides, and besides:
I will be your Muristan✿ Man
A cross-section of affection
Bustling with white hot feeling
For, since we met on Mount Moriah
Our heat's been raging like the altar's fire!

✿ Farsi: Hospital; a main thoroughfare in the Christian quarter of
Jerusalem's Old City

Girl of Katamon✿

There was a ground floor girl on HaPalmach Street
Whose touch was sweet and warming
We used to stroll for starlit soul
Sitting in parks, cautiously hand-in-hand
Wondering how we could make this work
Make this thrive alive and blessed
Kissed by longevity's moistened lips

God, how I'll miss her hand on my heart
Endless nights in the silent dark
With her head on my chest
Funny and naughty she called me always
First hours flew by then days
So much undeniably right
I'd been searching all my life
Someone to bathe in my ocean of adoration
I'd found her beautiful face and basked in it

Yet high walls of religion kept our love at bay
Our flaming blaze only blackened doctrine's stone
And now alone once more I remain
Sore and stained by the ash of heartbreak
My heart's mistake another lesson learned
Some ignorant others may well suppose
Nay and No Way! I say
The heart makes no mistakes, best believe!
For never is it in error
To unburden affection's bearer
To do away with pretenses
To drop one's defenses
And give in to love

✿ Greek: Near the monastery (San Simon); a once Greek and now
Jewish neighbourhood in West Jerusalem, a.k.a. Gonen

REVERIE

Winged Lions

Like vivid dreams in stolid statue form
Eternal feline seraphim claw into time
Scratching and biting fear into adversarial hearts

Safeguarding fortune with ferocious fervor
Loyal legionnaires in stone flank the holy throne
Defending sanctity from wild profane powers

In a Dream of the Night

Dark delight to illumine evening's action
I slew haunting demons with saber afire
To the twang of the lyre I resuscitated piety
Delivering comeuppance with express execution
Wreaking reckonings with hapless offenders
Defanged and impotent within imagination's chambers
Unaccepted atonements fell pathetically by the wayside
Summary justice dispensed with finite precision
Brooking no insolence from black rogues rendered inept
I slept soundly with a smile as fantasy flowed freely
Before the cock's crow I set matters aright
And lashed out with might against errant transgressors
Morning found me satiated with the sap of dead foes
Relishing vicarious victories in night vision's dimension

PRAYER

Rain in the Valley of Dry Bones

On this day I fervently pray for a flood of sophistication
To blot out the memory of a degenerate generation
Bring urgent emancipation to spirituality's station
Wash off the tongues of incivility's vibration
Cleanse discourtesy from interpersonal interaction
Deluge gentility to a sensitive heart's satisfaction
Bathe these inhabitants in waters of revelation
Baptize those sinners in the river of contemplation
Anoint the penitent with vessels of ablution
Consecrate the contrite in the spirit of resolution
Replenish the goodwill in each act and situation
Purify this people of unfeeling inconsideration!

A Root from a Desert Land

A rare root from a dry desert land cries out for salvation
Like a fugitive Messiah escaping inertia's wilderness
Hoping for allies and encouraging recognition
From kindred spirits whose clarity is keen

May the wind and the rain conspire to consecrate
That lonely soldier in the midst of stagnation
Status quo guardians obstructing obvious progress
Yet the light of righteous wisdom elevates until elation

Kaifeng, Hunan Province

To the Jew in Kaifeng, in Cochin and Kerala
Reach out to me from exile and I will reach out to you
Together our stretching arms will form a chuppah✿ in the Diaspora
Over the Holy Land of our mothers and fathers
A sukkah✿ over the Land of Israel spanning from east to west and back
All we have is each other
All we have is one another
Let us have each other
...and let us say Amen

✿ Hebrew: Marriage canopy
✿ Hebrew: Booth for the annual Festival of Tabernacles

May It Be Your Will

We will be like dreamers
Our mouths filled with laughter
Our tongues with glad song

We will march forward with ease
Our feet will not falter in the night
Our step will not stumble by day

We will be catapulted onto spiritual summits
Our souls will not become spiritually stagnant
Our hearts will scale heights rising heavenward

Praiseworthy is the worldly warrior
Who fills his quiver with the arrows of the Almighty
Who summons his soldiers with the blast of the shofar

For if He will not build the house
In vain do its laborers construct it!
If He will not guard the city
In vain are the watchmen vigilant!

More than once were we worthy, may we be so still
More than once we earned mercy, may it be Your will